# I Write to Win Journal

*That's my story...*

# THIS BOOK BELONGS TO:

_____

_____

_____

Dear Reader,

I wanted to create this journal as a tool for personal growth and self-reflection. Life can be fast-paced and overwhelming, and it's easy to lose sight of our true selves amidst the chaos. This journal serves as a space where you can reconnect with your inner thoughts, emotions, and desires.

I believe that self-reflection is essential for personal development. By taking the time to explore our thoughts and feelings, we gain a deeper understanding of ourselves and our needs.

Additionally, I wanted to create a journal that promotes gratitude and positivity. In our busy lives, it's crucial to pause and appreciate the blessings we have. Through daily gratitude practice, we can shift our focus towards the positive aspects of life and cultivate a mindset of abundance.

Ultimately, this journal is a tool for empowerment. It encourages you to take control of your journey, set intentions, and work towards personal growth. It's a reminder that you have the power to shape your life, embrace your true self, and find joy in the present moment. It equips you to win!

I hope this journal becomes a valuable companion on your path to self-discovery, gratitude, and personal transformation.

It's your winning season,
Tracey

Welcome to the best 12 weeks of your life!

Instructions and a winning affirmation start each week to prepare you and set the tone for you to share your thoughts and desires of growth and prosperity.

Start by using positive words to describe who you are; i.e. blessed, powerful, prosperous, healed, valuable, smart, physically and mentally whole, healthy, wealthy, and wise.

Take time to journal daily to release your thoughts. At the end of the week, take time to reflect on what you are grateful for.

Take an account for your daily activities on your *YOU DID IT* page as it helps you create a space of gratitude by clearing your mind and creating healthy habits.
- Did you workout each day to release stress and improve your health?
- Did you drink enough water or hydrate each day?
- Did you meditate each day?

If so, congratulations! If not, why? Hold yourself accountable for being the best version of you!

Make sure to write down your personal affirmations each week. Read and reread them throughout your journey.

Congratulations on taking steps to inspire yourself to be the BEST version of YOU!

# Week 1

- Carve out a dedicated slot in your daily routine, whether it's the serene morning or the contemplative evening, to engage with your journal of triumph.

- Begin by chronicling three victories you've savored over the past 24 hours. They may range from grand achievements to the simplest pleasures.

- Delve into the underlying reasons that spark your gratitude for each entry. Capture a sentence or two illuminating the affirmative influence it has woven into the tapestry of your life.

I am a capable and resilient person, capable of overcoming any challenge that comes my way.

"The greatest glory in living lies not in never falling, but in rising every time we fall."
— <u>Nelson Mandela</u>

# Daily

## Positive Words That Describe Who You Are

_____     _____
_____     _____
_____     _____
_____     _____
_____     _____
_____     _____
_____     _____

## BIG BOLD GOALS For This Week!

_____
_____
_____
_____
_____
_____
_____
_____
_____
_____
_____

# Week #1 _____

## Monday

---
---
---
---

## Tuesday

---
---
---
---

## Wednesday

---
---
---
---

## Thursday

---
---
---
---

## Friday

## Saturday

## Sunday

## Next Week

# Reflections:
## This week I am grateful for...

# You Did It!

| | MON | TUE | WED | THUR | FRI | SAT | SUN |
|---|---|---|---|---|---|---|---|
| **WORKOUT** | Yes, YOU did it! / __ No, Why not? | Yes, YOU did it! / __ No, Why not? | Yes, YOU did it! / __ No, Why not? | Yes, YOU did it! / __ No, Why not? | Yes, YOU did it! / __ No, Why not? | Yes, YOU did it! / __ No, Why not? | Yes, YOU did it! / __ No, Why not? |
| **HYDRATION** | Yes, YOU did it! / __ No, Why not? | Yes, YOU did it! / __ No, Why not? | Yes, YOU did it! / __ No, Why not? | Yes, YOU did it! / __ No, Why not? | Yes, YOU did it! / __ No, Why not? | Yes, YOU did it! / __ No, Why not? | Yes, YOU did it! / __ No, Why not? |
| **MEDITATION** | Yes, YOU did it! / __ No, Why not? | Yes, YOU did it! / __ No, Why not? | Yes, YOU did it! / __ No, Why not? | Yes, YOU did it! / __ No, Why not? | Yes, YOU did it! / __ No, Why not? | Yes, YOU did it! / __ No, Why not? | Yes, YOU did it! / __ No, Why not? |

# My Personal Affirmations

# Week 2

- Sustain the cherished practice of recording three daily blessings that grace your life.

- Push the boundaries of your gratitude exploration by seeking fresh and unique sources of appreciation every day.

- Stretch your gratitude journaling by crafting more vivid and intricate depictions of your gratitude subjects, immersing yourself in the sensory textures and emotions that these sources of gratitude evoke.

I am confident in my abilities and trust myself to make wise decisions.

*"The best way to find yourself is to lose yourself in the service of others."*
— *Mahatma Gandhi*

# Daily
Positive Words That Describe Who You Are

_____          _____
_____          _____
_____          _____
_____          _____
_____          _____
_____          _____
_____          _____

## BIG BOLD GOALS For This Week!

# Week #2_____

Monday

Tuesday

Wednesday

Thursday

## Friday

___

___

___

___

## Saturday

___

___

___

___

## Sunday

___

___

___

___

## Next Week

___

___

___

___

# Reflections:
## This week I am grateful for...

# You Did It!

| | MON | TUE | WED | THUR | FRI | SAT | SUN |
|---|---|---|---|---|---|---|---|
| **WORKOUT** | Yes, YOU did it! <br> __ No, Why not? | Yes, YOU did it! <br> __ No, Why not? | Yes, YOU did it! <br> __ No, Why not? | Yes, YOU did it! <br> __ No, Why not? | Yes, YOU did it! <br> __ No, Why not? | Yes, YOU did it! <br> __ No, Why not? | Yes, YOU did it! <br> __ No, Why not? |
| | MON | TUE | WED | THUR | FRI | SAT | SUN |
| **HYDRATION** | Yes, YOU did it! <br> __ No, Why not? | Yes, YOU did it! <br> __ No, Why not? | Yes, YOU did it! <br> __ No, Why not? | Yes, YOU did it! <br> __ No, Why not? | Yes, YOU did it! <br> __ No, Why not? | Yes, YOU did it! <br> __ No, Why not? | Yes, YOU did it! <br> __ No, Why not? |
| | MON | TUE | WED | THUR | FRI | SAT | SUN |
| **MEDITATION** | Yes, YOU did it! <br> __ No, Why not? | Yes, YOU did it! <br> __ No, Why not? | Yes, YOU did it! <br> __ No, Why not? | Yes, YOU did it! <br> __ No, Why not? | Yes, YOU did it! <br> __ No, Why not? | Yes, YOU did it! <br> __ No, Why not? | Yes, YOU did it! <br> __ No, Why not? |

# My Personal Affirmations

# Week 3

- Enhance your gratitude ritual by weaving gratitude for the people who illuminate your life.

- Jot down the names of three exceptional individuals who fill your heart with gratitude, and delve into the profound reasons that kindle your appreciation.

- Ponder the possibility of connecting with one of these cherished souls to convey your gratitude personally, letting your heartfelt words strengthen the bonds of gratitude and connection.

I am strong, both mentally and physically, and I continue to grow in strength every day.

"I am not interested in picking up crumbs of compassion thrown from the table of someone who considers himself my master. I want the full menu of rights."
— <u>Archbishop Desmond Tutu</u>

# Daily

## Positive Words That Describe Who You Are

_____     _____
_____     _____
_____     _____
_____     _____
_____     _____
_____     _____
_____     _____

## BIG BOLD GOALS For This Week!

_____
_____
_____
_____
_____
_____
_____
_____
_____
_____
_____
_____

# Week #3 _____

Monday
_____
_____
_____
_____

Tuesday
_____
_____
_____
_____

Wednesday
_____
_____
_____
_____

Thursday
_____
_____
_____
_____

## Friday

## Saturday

## Sunday

## Next Week

# Reflections:
# This week I am grateful for...

# You Did It!

| | MON | TUE | WED | THUR | FRI | SAT | SUN |
|---|---|---|---|---|---|---|---|
| **WORKOUT** | Yes, YOU did it! <br> __ No, Why not? | Yes, YOU did it! <br> __ No, Why not? | Yes, YOU did it! <br> __ No, Why not? | Yes, YOU did it! <br> __ No, Why not? | Yes, YOU did it! <br> __ No, Why not? | Yes, YOU did it! <br> __ No, Why not? | Yes, YOU did it! <br> __ No, Why not? |
| **HYDRATION** | Yes, YOU did it! <br> __ No, Why not? | Yes, YOU did it! <br> __ No, Why not? | Yes, YOU did it! <br> __ No, Why not? | Yes, YOU did it! <br> __ No, Why not? | Yes, YOU did it! <br> __ No, Why not? | Yes, YOU did it! <br> __ No, Why not? | Yes, YOU did it! <br> __ No, Why not? |
| **MEDITATION** | Yes, YOU did it! <br> __ No, Why not? | Yes, YOU did it! <br> __ No, Why not? | Yes, YOU did it! <br> __ No, Why not? | Yes, YOU did it! <br> __ No, Why not? | Yes, YOU did it! <br> __ No, Why not? | Yes, YOU did it! <br> __ No, Why not? | Yes, YOU did it! <br> __ No, Why not? |

# My Personal Affirmations

# Week 4

- Pause to contemplate the last month of diligent journaling. Observe any recurrent motifs or themes threading through your entries.

- Select one gem from your previous records that stirs an especially profound sense of gratitude, and extend your thoughts into a more elaborate and descriptive entry.

- Reflect upon how the act of expressing gratitude has influenced your general mindset and well-being.

I am a source of love, support, and inspiration for my family and friends.

*"Gratitude opens the door to the power, the wisdom, the creativity of the universe. You open the door through gratitude."*
— Deepak Chopra

# Daily
## Positive Words That Describe Who You Are

_____        _____
_____        _____
_____        _____
_____        _____
_____        _____
_____        _____
_____        _____

## BIG BOLD GOALS For This Week!

_____
_____
_____
_____
_____
_____
_____
_____
_____
_____
_____
_____
_____

# Week #4 _____

Monday
_____
_____
_____
_____

Tuesday
_____
_____
_____
_____

Wednesday
_____
_____
_____
_____

Thursday
_____
_____
_____
_____

## Friday

_____
_____
_____
_____

## Saturday

_____
_____
_____
_____

## Sunday

_____
_____
_____
_____

## Next Week

_____
_____
_____
_____

# Reflections:
## This week I am grateful for...

# You Did It!

| | MON | TUE | WED | THUR | FRI | SAT | SUN |
|---|---|---|---|---|---|---|---|
| **WORKOUT** | Yes, YOU did it! <br> __ No, Why not? | Yes, YOU did it! <br> __ No, Why not? | Yes, YOU did it! <br> __ No, Why not? | Yes, YOU did it! <br> __ No, Why not? | Yes, YOU did it! <br> __ No, Why not? | Yes, YOU did it! <br> __ No, Why not? | Yes, YOU did it! <br> __ No, Why not? |
| **HYDRATION** | Yes, YOU did it! <br> __ No, Why not? | Yes, YOU did it! <br> __ No, Why not? | Yes, YOU did it! <br> __ No, Why not? | Yes, YOU did it! <br> __ No, Why not? | Yes, YOU did it! <br> __ No, Why not? | Yes, YOU did it! <br> __ No, Why not? | Yes, YOU did it! <br> __ No, Why not? |
| **MEDITATION** | Yes, YOU did it! <br> __ No, Why not? | Yes, YOU did it! <br> __ No, Why not? | Yes, YOU did it! <br> __ No, Why not? | Yes, YOU did it! <br> __ No, Why not? | Yes, YOU did it! <br> __ No, Why not? | Yes, YOU did it! <br> __ No, Why not? | Yes, YOU did it! <br> __ No, Why not? |

# My Personal Affirmations

# Week 5

- Discover the strength of gratitude for the great outdoors and our environment. Jot down three natural wonders that inspire your gratitude.

- Zoom in on distinctive features, such as the rugged majesty of a mountain peak, the untamed roar of ocean waves, or the earthy scent of a forest after rainfall.

- Allocate a few moments daily to forge a bond with nature and magnify your reverence for the wonders of the wild.

I am in control of my emotions and respond to life's ups and downs with grace and composure.

"I will love the light for it shows me the way, yet I will endure the darkness because it shows me the stars."
— Og Mandino

# Daily

Positive Words That Describe Who You Are

_____         _____
_____         _____
_____         _____
_____         _____
_____         _____
_____         _____
_____         _____

## BIG BOLD GOALS For This Week!

_____
_____
_____
_____
_____
_____
_____
_____
_____
_____
_____
_____

# Week #5 _____

Monday
___
___
___
___

Tuesday
___
___
___
___

Wednesday
___
___
___
___

Thursday
___
___
___
___

## Friday

---
---
---
---

## Saturday

---
---
---
---

## Sunday

---
---
---
---

## Next Week

---
---
---
---

# Reflections:
## This week I am grateful for...

# You Did It!

| | MON | TUE | WED | THUR | FRI | SAT | SUN |
|---|---|---|---|---|---|---|---|
| **WORKOUT** | Yes, YOU did it! <br> __ No, Why not? | Yes, YOU did it! <br> __ No, Why not? | Yes, YOU did it! <br> __ No, Why not? | Yes, YOU did it! <br> __ No, Why not? | Yes, YOU did it! <br> __ No, Why not? | Yes, YOU did it! <br> __ No, Why not? | Yes, YOU did it! <br> __ No, Why not? |
| **HYDRATION** | Yes, YOU did it! <br> __ No, Why not? | Yes, YOU did it! <br> __ No, Why not? | Yes, YOU did it! <br> __ No, Why not? | Yes, YOU did it! <br> __ No, Why not? | Yes, YOU did it! <br> __ No, Why not? | Yes, YOU did it! <br> __ No, Why not? | Yes, YOU did it! <br> __ No, Why not? |
| **MEDITATION** | Yes, YOU did it! <br> __ No, Why not? | Yes, YOU did it! <br> __ No, Why not? | Yes, YOU did it! <br> __ No, Why not? | Yes, YOU did it! <br> __ No, Why not? | Yes, YOU did it! <br> __ No, Why not? | Yes, YOU did it! <br> __ No, Why not? | Yes, YOU did it! <br> __ No, Why not? |

# My Personal Affirmations

# Week 6

- During this week, pivot your attention toward gratitude for the marvel that is your body and your health.

- Capture three facets of your physical well-being that ignite your gratitude.

- Contemplate how your body serves as the vessel through which you partake in activities, savor life's pleasures, and navigate the intricate terrain of this world.

I am a leader, and I lead with integrity, empathy, and authenticity.

"What separates privilege from entitlement is gratitude."
— <u>Brené Brown</u>

# Daily
## Positive Words That Describe Who You Are

_____        _____
_____        _____
_____        _____
_____        _____
_____        _____
_____        _____
_____        _____

## BIG BOLD GOALS For This Week!

_____
_____
_____
_____
_____
_____
_____
_____
_____
_____
_____
_____

# Week #6 _____

## Monday
___
___
___
___

## Tuesday
___
___
___
___

## Wednesday
___
___
___
___

## Thursday
___
___
___
___

## Friday

---
---
---
---

## Saturday

---
---
---
---

## Sunday

---
---
---
---

## Next Week

---
---
---
---

# Reflections:
# This week I am grateful for...

# You Did It!

| | MON | TUE | WED | THUR | FRI | SAT | SUN |
|---|---|---|---|---|---|---|---|
| **WORKOUT** | Yes, YOU did it! <br> __ No, Why not? | Yes, YOU did it! <br> __ No, Why not? | Yes, YOU did it! <br> __ No, Why not? | Yes, YOU did it! <br> __ No, Why not? | Yes, YOU did it! <br> __ No, Why not? | Yes, YOU did it! <br> __ No, Why not? | Yes, YOU did it! <br> __ No, Why not? |
| **HYDRATION** | Yes, YOU did it! <br> __ No, Why not? | Yes, YOU did it! <br> __ No, Why not? | Yes, YOU did it! <br> __ No, Why not? | Yes, YOU did it! <br> __ No, Why not? | Yes, YOU did it! <br> __ No, Why not? | Yes, YOU did it! <br> __ No, Why not? | Yes, YOU did it! <br> __ No, Why not? |
| **MEDITATION** | Yes, YOU did it! <br> __ No, Why not? | Yes, YOU did it! <br> __ No, Why not? | Yes, YOU did it! <br> __ No, Why not? | Yes, YOU did it! <br> __ No, Why not? | Yes, YOU did it! <br> __ No, Why not? | Yes, YOU did it! <br> __ No, Why not? | Yes, YOU did it! <br> __ No, Why not? |

# My Personal Affirmations

# Week 7

- Embrace gratitude for the gift of learning and personal evolution.

- Transcribe three fresh lessons you've acquired recently and illuminate why you cherish this newfound knowledge.

- Contemplate how this ongoing journey of learning enriches your personal growth, furnishing you with invaluable tools to navigate life's twists and turns with confidence and resilience.

I am worthy of success and abundance, and I attract prosperity into my life.

*"You are not what you've done. You are what you keep doing."*
— *Jack Butcher*

# Daily
## Positive Words That Describe Who You Are

_____   _____
_____   _____
_____   _____
_____   _____
_____   _____
_____   _____
_____   _____

## BIG BOLD GOALS For This Week!

_____
_____
_____
_____
_____
_____
_____
_____
_____
_____
_____

# Week #7 _____

## Monday

## Tuesday

## Wednesday

## Thursday

## Friday

---
---
---
---

## Saturday

---
---
---
---

## Sunday

---
---
---
---

## Next Week

---
---
---
---

# Reflections:
## This week I am grateful for...

# You Did It!

|  | MON | TUE | WED | THUR | FRI | SAT | SUN |
|---|---|---|---|---|---|---|---|
| **WORKOUT** | Yes, YOU did it! | Yes, YOU did it! | Yes, YOU did it! | Yes, YOU did it! | Yes, YOU did it! | Yes, YOU did it! | Yes, YOU did it! |
|  | __ No, Why not? | __ No, Why not? | __ No, Why not? | __ No, Why not? | __ No, Why not? | __ No, Why not? | __ No, Why not? |
| **HYDRATION** | Yes, YOU did it! | Yes, YOU did it! | Yes, YOU did it! | Yes, YOU did it! | Yes, YOU did it! | Yes, YOU did it! | Yes, YOU did it! |
|  | __ No, Why not? | __ No, Why not? | __ No, Why not? | __ No, Why not? | __ No, Why not? | __ No, Why not? | __ No, Why not? |
| **MEDITATION** | Yes, YOU did it! | Yes, YOU did it! | Yes, YOU did it! | Yes, YOU did it! | Yes, YOU did it! | Yes, YOU did it! | Yes, YOU did it! |
|  | __ No, Why not? | __ No, Why not? | __ No, Why not? | __ No, Why not? | __ No, Why not? | __ No, Why not? | __ No, Why not? |

# My Personal Affirmations

# Week 8

- Nurture gratitude for life's uncomplicated delights.

- Jot down three modest, everyday sources of joy and gratitude that grace your existence.

- Dedicate yourself to full presence, savoring these fleeting moments of simplicity and pleasure as they unfurl throughout your day.

I am constantly improving and evolving as a person, embracing opportunities for personal growth.

*"The love and attention you always thought you wanted from someone else, is the love and attention you first need to give to yourself."*
— Bryant McGillns

# Daily
## Positive Words That Describe Who You Are

_____     _____
_____     _____
_____     _____
_____     _____
_____     _____
_____     _____

## BIG BOLD GOALS For This Week!

_____
_____
_____
_____
_____
_____
_____
_____
_____
_____
_____

# Week #8 _____

Monday
_____
_____
_____
_____

Tuesday
_____
_____
_____
_____

Wednesday
_____
_____
_____
_____

Thursday
_____
_____
_____
_____

## Friday

_____
_____
_____
_____

## Saturday

_____
_____
_____
_____

## Sunday

_____
_____
_____
_____

## Next Week

_____
_____
_____
_____

# Reflections:
# This week I am grateful for...

# You Did It!

| | MON | TUE | WED | THUR | FRI | SAT | SUN |
|---|---|---|---|---|---|---|---|
| **WORKOUT** | Yes, YOU did it! <br> __ No, Why not? | Yes, YOU did it! <br> __ No, Why not? | Yes, YOU did it! <br> __ No, Why not? | Yes, YOU did it! <br> __ No, Why not? | Yes, YOU did it! <br> __ No, Why not? | Yes, YOU did it! <br> __ No, Why not? | Yes, YOU did it! <br> __ No, Why not? |
| **HYDRATION** | Yes, YOU did it! <br> __ No, Why not? | Yes, YOU did it! <br> __ No, Why not? | Yes, YOU did it! <br> __ No, Why not? | Yes, YOU did it! <br> __ No, Why not? | Yes, YOU did it! <br> __ No, Why not? | Yes, YOU did it! <br> __ No, Why not? | Yes, YOU did it! <br> __ No, Why not? |
| **MEDITATION** | Yes, YOU did it! <br> __ No, Why not? | Yes, YOU did it! <br> __ No, Why not? | Yes, YOU did it! <br> __ No, Why not? | Yes, YOU did it! <br> __ No, Why not? | Yes, YOU did it! <br> __ No, Why not? | Yes, YOU did it! <br> __ No, Why not? | Yes, YOU did it! <br> __ No, Why not? |

# My Personal Affirmations

# Week 9

- Direct your gratitude lens towards the precious tapestry of relationships and social bonds.

- Record three individuals whose presence has cast a luminous influence on your life, elucidating why you hold their presence in such high regard.

- Ponder the avenues through which you can cultivate and fortify these connections as you journey forward, weaving deeper threads of appreciation into your social fabric.

I am kind, compassionate, and respectful in all my interactions with others.

"Even if it makes others uncomfortable, I will love who I am."
— Janelle Monáe

# Daily
## Positive Words That Describe Who You Are

_____      _____
_____      _____
_____      _____
_____      _____
_____      _____
_____      _____
_____      _____

## BIG BOLD GOALS For This Week!

_____
_____
_____
_____
_____
_____
_____
_____
_____
_____
_____
_____
_____

# Week #9 _____

Monday
_____
_____
_____
_____

Tuesday
_____
_____
_____
_____

Wednesday
_____
_____
_____
_____

Thursday
_____
_____
_____
_____

## Friday

_____
_____
_____
_____

## Saturday

_____
_____
_____
_____

## Sunday

_____
_____
_____
_____

## Next Week

_____
_____
_____
_____

# Reflections:
## This week I am grateful for...

# You Did It!

| | MON | TUE | WED | THUR | FRI | SAT | SUN |
|---|---|---|---|---|---|---|---|
| **WORKOUT** | Yes, YOU did it! | Yes, YOU did it! | Yes, YOU did it! | Yes, YOU did it! | Yes, YOU did it! | Yes, YOU did it! | Yes, YOU did it! |
| | __ No, Why not? | __ No, Why not? | __ No, Why not? | __ No, Why not? | __ No, Why not? | __ No, Why not? | __ No, Why not? |
| | MON | TUE | WED | THUR | FRI | SAT | SUN |
| **HYDRATION** | Yes, YOU did it! | Yes, YOU did it! | Yes, YOU did it! | Yes, YOU did it! | Yes, YOU did it! | Yes, YOU did it! | Yes, YOU did it! |
| | __ No, Why not? | __ No, Why not? | __ No, Why not? | __ No, Why not? | __ No, Why not? | __ No, Why not? | __ No, Why not? |
| | MON | TUE | WED | THUR | FRI | SAT | SUN |
| **MEDITATION** | Yes, YOU did it! | Yes, YOU did it! | Yes, YOU did it! | Yes, YOU did it! | Yes, YOU did it! | Yes, YOU did it! | Yes, YOU did it! |
| | __ No, Why not? | __ No, Why not? | __ No, Why not? | __ No, Why not? | __ No, Why not? | __ No, Why not? | __ No, Why not? |

# My Personal Affirmations

# Week 10

- Embark on a voyage of gratitude for your achievements and feats.

- Document three goals or milestones you've triumphantly reached, and let your words overflow with gratitude for the sweat and toil you've invested.

- Commence a jubilant celebration of your successes, taking a moment to bask in the glow of your accomplishments and recognize the strides you've made along your path.

I am open to new experiences and adventures that bring joy and excitement into my life.

*"I am not what happened to me, I am what I choose to become."*
— *Carl Gustav Jung*

# Daily

## Positive Words That Describe Who You Are

_____    _____
_____    _____
_____    _____
_____    _____
_____    _____
_____    _____
_____    _____

## BIG BOLD GOALS For This Week!

_____
_____
_____
_____
_____
_____
_____
_____
_____
_____
_____

# Week #10 _____

Monday
___
___
___
___

Tuesday
___
___
___
___

Wednesday
___
___
___
___

Thursday
___
___
___
___

## Friday

## Saturday

## Sunday

## Next Week

# Reflections:
## This week I am grateful for...

# You Did It!

## WORKOUT

| MON | TUE | WED | THUR | FRI | SAT | SUN |
|---|---|---|---|---|---|---|
| Yes, YOU did it! | Yes, YOU did it! | Yes, YOU did it! | Yes, YOU did it! | Yes, YOU did it! | Yes, YOU did it! | Yes, YOU did it! |
| __ No, Why not? | __ No, Why not? | __ No, Why not? | __ No, Why not? | __ No, Why not? | __ No, Why not? | __ No, Why not? |

## HYDRATION

| MON | TUE | WED | THUR | FRI | SAT | SUN |
|---|---|---|---|---|---|---|
| Yes, YOU did it! | Yes, YOU did it! | Yes, YOU did it! | Yes, YOU did it! | Yes, YOU did it! | Yes, YOU did it! | Yes, YOU did it! |
| __ No, Why not? | __ No, Why not? | __ No, Why not? | __ No, Why not? | __ No, Why not? | __ No, Why not? | __ No, Why not? |

## MEDITATION

| MON | TUE | WED | THUR | FRI | SAT | SUN |
|---|---|---|---|---|---|---|
| Yes, YOU did it! | Yes, YOU did it! | Yes, YOU did it! | Yes, YOU did it! | Yes, YOU did it! | Yes, YOU did it! | Yes, YOU did it! |
| __ No, Why not? | __ No, Why not? | __ No, Why not? | __ No, Why not? | __ No, Why not? | __ No, Why not? | __ No, Why not? |

# My Personal Affirmations

# Week 11

- During this week, turn your gratitude inward, celebrating your inner strengths and qualities.

- Articulate three personal qualities or traits that resonate with your appreciation.

- Contemplate the profound impact of these strengths on your journey, how they've fortified your resolve, helped you conquer obstacles, and nurtured your growth as an individual.

I am a positive role model for those around me, inspiring them to be their best selves.

*"I am stronger than my challenges, and my challenges are making me stronger."*
— Karen Salmansohn

# Daily

## Positive Words That Describe Who You Are

_____    _____
_____    _____
_____    _____
_____    _____
_____    _____
_____    _____
_____    _____

## BIG BOLD GOALS For This Week!

_____
_____
_____
_____
_____
_____
_____
_____
_____
_____
_____

# Week #11 _____

Monday
___
___
___
___

Tuesday
___
___
___
___

Wednesday
___
___
___
___

Thursday
___
___
___
___

## Friday

---
---
---
---

## Saturday

---
---
---
---

## Sunday

---
---
---
---

## Next Week

---
---
---
---

# Reflections:
## This week I am grateful for...

# You Did It!

| | MON | TUE | WED | THUR | FRI | SAT | SUN |
|---|---|---|---|---|---|---|---|
| **WORKOUT** | Yes, YOU did it! __ No, Why not? | Yes, YOU did it! __ No, Why not? | Yes, YOU did it! __ No, Why not? | Yes, YOU did it! __ No, Why not? | Yes, YOU did it! __ No, Why not? | Yes, YOU did it! __ No, Why not? | Yes, YOU did it! __ No, Why not? |
| **HYDRATION** | Yes, YOU did it! __ No, Why not? | Yes, YOU did it! __ No, Why not? | Yes, YOU did it! __ No, Why not? | Yes, YOU did it! __ No, Why not? | Yes, YOU did it! __ No, Why not? | Yes, YOU did it! __ No, Why not? | Yes, YOU did it! __ No, Why not? |
| **MEDITATION** | Yes, YOU did it! __ No, Why not? | Yes, YOU did it! __ No, Why not? | Yes, YOU did it! __ No, Why not? | Yes, YOU did it! __ No, Why not? | Yes, YOU did it! __ No, Why not? | Yes, YOU did it! __ No, Why not? | Yes, YOU did it! __ No, Why not? |

# My Personal Affirmations

# Week 12

- Take a moment to reflect on your journaling experience, the mindset transformation, and heightened awareness of the abundance in your life.

- Write a summary of your overall experience, including any significant insights or changes you have noticed in your mindset.

- Make it a priority to:
    - Continue daily journaling,
    - Express gratitude daily, and
    - Meditate.

- As you complete this 12-week journaling practice, do so with a heart full of gratitude and a commitment to continue growing through the practice of appreciating life's blessings.

I am grateful for the blessings in my life and look forward to a future filled with happiness and fulfillment.

"Believe in yourself and all that you are. Know that there is something inside you that is greater than any obstacle."
— Christian D. Larson

# Daily

## Positive Words That Describe Who You Are

_____    _____
_____    _____
_____    _____
_____    _____
_____    _____
_____    _____
_____    _____

## BIG BOLD GOALS For This Week!

_____
_____
_____
_____
_____
_____
_____
_____
_____
_____
_____
_____

# Week #1_____

Monday
_____
_____
_____
_____

Tuesday
_____
_____
_____
_____

Wednesday
_____
_____
_____
_____

Thursday
_____
_____
_____
_____

Friday
_____
_____
_____
_____

Saturday
_____
_____
_____
_____

Sunday
_____
_____
_____
_____

Next Week
_____
_____
_____
_____

# Reflections:
## This week I am grateful for...

# You Did It!

## WORKOUT

| MON | TUE | WED | THUR | FRI | SAT | SUN |
|---|---|---|---|---|---|---|
| Yes, YOU did it! | Yes, YOU did it! | Yes, YOU did it! | Yes, YOU did it! | Yes, YOU did it! | Yes, YOU did it! | Yes, YOU did it! |
| __ No, Why not? | __ No, Why not? | __ No, Why not? | __ No, Why not? | __ No, Why not? | __ No, Why not? | __ No, Why not? |

## HYDRATION

| MON | TUE | WED | THUR | FRI | SAT | SUN |
|---|---|---|---|---|---|---|
| Yes, YOU did it! | Yes, YOU did it! | Yes, YOU did it! | Yes, YOU did it! | Yes, YOU did it! | Yes, YOU did it! | Yes, YOU did it! |
| __ No, Why not? | __ No, Why not? | __ No, Why not? | __ No, Why not? | __ No, Why not? | __ No, Why not? | __ No, Why not? |

## MEDITATION

| MON | TUE | WED | THUR | FRI | SAT | SUN |
|---|---|---|---|---|---|---|
| Yes, YOU did it! | Yes, YOU did it! | Yes, YOU did it! | Yes, YOU did it! | Yes, YOU did it! | Yes, YOU did it! | Yes, YOU did it! |
| __ No, Why not? | __ No, Why not? | __ No, Why not? | __ No, Why not? | __ No, Why not? | __ No, Why not? | __ No, Why not? |

# My Personal Affirmations

www.ingramcontent.com/pod-product-compliance
Lightning Source LLC
Chambersburg PA
CBHW051129050526
R18244800001B/R182448PG44119CBX00002B/1